Juliet Nicolson worked in publishing in England and the United States before becoming a writer and journalist. She has written two works of non-fiction which bookend the First World War: *The Perfect Summer: Dancing into Shadow in 1911* and *The Great Silence: 1918–1920 Living in the Shadow of the Great War*. Her first novel, *Abdication*, is set in England in 1936 and was published by Bloomsbury in 2012. She lives with her husband in East Sussex.

Works by the same author

Non-fiction

The Perfect Summer:
Dancing into Shadow in 1911

The Great Silence:
1918–1920 Living in the Shadow
of the Great War

Fiction

Abdication

MEMORY
and
DESIRE

JULIET NICOLSON

Published by The Cuckoo Press
for John Sandoe (Books) Ltd
10 Blacklands Terrace, London SW3 2SR

A CIP catalogue reference for this book
is available from the British Library

ISBN 978 0 9566444 2 8

Designed by Fenella Willis

Printed and bound in the UK by Antony Rowe Ltd
Bumper's Farm, Chippenham, Wiltshire

For Jeremy Hutchinson
with much love

MEMORY AND DESIRE

There is a box hedge in the garden where I grew up which reaches to just above my knees. If I crouch down beside the hedge so that my hand is level with the top, close my eyes, and run my fingers along the feathery surface, the sensation returns me at once to my seven-year-old self. There are other parts of the garden that have the power to efface time: a tiny sunken courtyard filled with giant lilies into which we would vanish as soon as lunch was ready, infuriating the adults, and a narrow brick path that winds along the side of an old wooden hut where gardening tools are still kept. As you press down the latch of the hut door, leaving the smell of honeysuckle to suffuse the air outside, and adjust your eyes to the darkness, the shapes of rusted iron spades gradually strengthen into focus, their smooth wooden handles hanging on nails tacked into the beams. Beside them are dangerous-looking, sharp-pronged forks; and, propped against the wall, an ingenious wooden seat with chipped green metal handle bars, ideal for sitting on to weed or, when turned upside down, for standing on to prune out-of-reach roses. If I stand now for a moment on that seat and grip the roughly painted handles in my palms, I can take myself back half a century.

Truly valuable memories, the kind that deliver an instant punch of return to a single moment long ago, are not always prompted by photograph albums or brought back by some elusive mental struggle to remember the detail of the past. Cleaner, more rounded recollections come rushing at you from embedded sensations: a taste, touch, smell, sight or sound that perhaps seemed insignificant at the time, but can be ignited unexpectedly decades later by the simplest of experiences.

It is Proust, of course, who best describes how memories are most effectively triggered by the senses rather than the intellect. 'The smell and taste of things remain poised a long time, like souls,' he writes in *Swann's Way,* the first book of *A La Recherche du Temps Perdu*, 'ready to remind us, waiting and hoping for their moment, amid the ruins of all the rest.' The hippocampus – the area of the brain where all sensory information is gathered and processed – ensures, for example, that if the taste-trigger is activated, then some or all of the other neighbouring senses will respond and deliver a rounded, visualised and amplified memory. It is as if the entire body of some formidable sea creature lying somnolent beneath a muddy surface can be stirred into action by the simple tweak of his tail.

During childhood and adolescence one's mind is at its most energetic, gathering and storing away these sense-sensitive experiences like bees in a hive, ready for the adult to return to discover the nectar, sometimes deliberately, sometimes involuntarily. These memories that are created during youth become those that are most intensely precious at the end, when life begins to ebb away. This layer of unconsciously amassed credit repays those conscious dividends years later. 'It is the things in life that you *don't* do' was a family saying drummed into us children from the earliest age. An existence deficient in the great experiences – be they practical, such as travel, or emotional, especially love – can become at the final moment an existence void of memories that prompts the incurable pain of regret. Memories, whether those of an individual or celebrated collectively by a group, can become a source of consolation in moments of despair or doubt, providing validation that one has lived a rich and varied life. The retrieval of the past is a process to be relished, wherein the unexpected recollection of long-neglected experiences resembles the discovery of old home movies abandoned in the attic. I am interested not only in the way memory plays its part during life but in the inestimably valuable pay-out during the last phase of all.

Smells associated with early childhood are powerful time capsules. The medicinal scent of a bar of golden, transparent Pears soap evokes, for me, a grandfather who allowed his grandchildren to be present during his morning shave and whose conversation was funnier than that of any other adult we knew. My memory-prompts of school a few years later relate more to foods and tastes that are not always enjoyable to revisit. Grey hunks of liver with unswallowable whitish pipes threaded through the centre and puddings made with cereals have ensured that offal and tapioca are never now part of our menu at home. Eggs too, especially the fried kind with their metallic-tasting, over-cooked, frilly edges, have joined my private list of bile-inducing foods. I can never forget or forgive the way the sticky yellow seepage of the yolk onto the crispy fried bread contaminated the only palatable ingredient of the horrid, compulsory, pre-communion Sunday school breakfast. Simultaneous in timescale, but an antidote to the life-long egg and tapioca prejudice, is the unfailingly delicious flavour of avocado and its attendant creamy, sugary dressing, served as an exotic welcome-home treat by my mother at the beginning of the holidays. By contrast, roast chicken, associated with the ritualistic last lunch before returning to boarding school, fails even now to deliver much pleasure.

In order to live, one must eat. Like the act of procreation itself, this biological necessity can involve all five of the senses. Perhaps that is why food and sex remain so important in reveries of former times. It is no coincidence that people whose own reproductive capability is long gone find a particular pleasure in the sensory delights integral to growing flowers, fruit and vegetables.

For my grown-up children, the sound of pop-corn popping beneath the lid of a deep pan promises a night at home watching favourite movies, just as it did when they were small. For me the carefree contentment of distant English summers is contained within the sweet smell of mint in a boiling pan of new potatoes; the sight of a perfectly poached, velvety-pink salmon; the sensation of the first slim, slippery stems of asparagus in my hand; the taste of a mouthful of just-picked, home-grown, still-dewy raspberries. It is hardly surprising that the last meals chosen by those awaiting execution in places where the death penalty still applies attract such intense fascination. A set of photographs in a recent colour supplement provoked many questions. What innocent time was a convicted assassin recalling when he asked for a final feast of coral-coloured lobster, followed by a slice of apple pie and cream? What was on the mind of a villainous woman hours away from a fatal injection who requested a fresh peach, as luscious as any immortalised on a Chardin canvas? Was *he* remembering the innocence of seaside holidays long ago? Was *she* recalling the soft bloom of a mother's cheek? Was there some secret joke contained within the single black olive ordered by a third individual, also destined for the electric chair? Did he hope the taste would help erase the reality of his fate and return him to a moment when laughter was an appropriate response to life?

Revisiting places one has worked in, lived in or briefly visited can be fundamental to the recollection of an entire period of one's life. One of the most evocative smells of my teenage years still exists in the Times Room in the basement of the London Library in St James's Square. More than half a lifetime ago I would descend the wooden stairs to spend university holidays in my part-time research role, checking off my father's lists of footnote queries for the latest volume of diaries or letters that he was in the process of editing. Turning the old broadsheet pages, taking care not to tear the fragile edges, I would check for dates of births, marriages and deaths, noting down illuminating obituaries, details of violent weather, spellings of obscure names. Even now, when heaving the huge red leather-bound volumes off the shelves and releasing the mustiness of centuries, I can revive my undergraduate excitement at discovering forgotten minutiae of history. I have long since found that walking myself visually up the stairs, along the corridors and even into the cupboards of houses I once lived in is a more efficient way of inducing sleep than meandering round a field of indistinguishable sheep. Sometimes the detail of those rooms comes back to me. A new book in which the pages have not yet been cut, a pot of emerald nail polish, a frayed velvet cushion in a stranger's hallway or an overeager electric hotplate in an overheated dining room can all resurrect the mood of a past life. But just as Proust cautions that the memory-jogging taste of a madeleine dipped in tea must be rationed if it is to retain its full power, I limit my nocturnal house travel to my most insomniac nights.

Smells and sights and sounds in places are capable of bringing back distant centuries. Visits to the battlefield of Hastings in the school holidays were accompanied by a parental suggestion that we close our eyes while standing among indifferent cows and listen to an agonised scream: our father's attempt to convince us how loudly poor King Harold must have yelled when the arrow hit his eye. About a mile from where I live in Sussex is a meadow that in mid-summer is bright with scattered buttercups. To reach this place one must climb high up onto the ridge of the South Downs past men flying kites, their shorts held up with *Swallows and Amazons* snake-clasp belts, before dipping steeply down through the cowslips and wild orchids flowering in the folds of the hills. On the meadow floor, rabbits race away for the sanctuary of their labyrinthine tunnels, bees hover over the promise of pollen-packed clover, and a pair of kestrels wheel above on the breeze, with an occasional languid movement of their wings. Far below them the frantic flapping of the sparrows slaps against the air's downward pull. Timelessness is in the very quality of the silence here. Shakespeare, Keats, Hardy, Lawrence and Kipling all saw, heard, smelled and touched a place like this.

The pleasure of experiencing and reading about identical sensations undergone by the greatest dramatists, poets, novelists, diarists and essayists of the past can bring tranquillity to a nation's fast-moving, anxiety-ridden soul. In Britain, at times of national mourning as well as celebration, those rousing patriotic favourites – the words and music of William Blake's and Hubert Parry's *Jerusalem*, Cecil Spring Rice's *I Vow to the My Country* and, of course, the National Anthem itself – sustained a nation through two world wars. They are the sounds that continue to unite us in song even if we do not agree with a single word of the sentiments. Familiar words, be they verses of hymns learned long ago and never forgotten, or passages from literature with which one has a lifelong acquaintance, have the power to transport one in time as powerfully as any photographic record. 'The great grey-green, greasy Limpopo River' beats out the alliterative drumroll of a childhood bedtime. Not long ago, at her memorial service, the recorded voice of my first inspiring English teacher jolted me back to the first time I heard Dickens read aloud. When my father became ill and took to his bed for the last time, he sometimes turned to his favourite books, finding their silent companionship preferable to human chatter. As an undergraduate he had bought at Blackwell's bookshop a leather-bound copy of *Wuthering Heights*, which he had kept all his life. On the back page in pencil he would make a careful annotation of each date on which he reread the book. There was a neat entry every five years. The final date was written just a few weeks before he died.

While researching three books, set variously just outside and just within living memory, one of my greatest pleasures has been to coax recollections from people who are unaware that what seem to be dreary quotidian activities, tucked into the pleats of a long life, become sparklers for a social historian. The process made me conscious of one of the few benefits of getting older. Again and again I came across those who had difficulty remembering events of a week ago but to whom, with a little prompting, the far distant past returned in ever-sharper focus.

An adored aunt was at first sceptical that the shopping trips to a department store she used to make with her mother in the 1920s could have any relevance to my book about the aftermath of the war. But when I explained my interest in the 'nearly new' top floor and lit up at her description of travelling for the first time in a lift, she opened up a little more. 'When I was twenty I had a Blackshirt for a boyfriend, you know,' she once said casually as she poured me a cup of tea. 'Not for long, mind you,' she assured me, stirring in the milk before looking up at me to check that I had got the point.

Last year on a hot English summer day, I was speaking in a muggy canvas tent to a group of people who were assembled there to hear tales of life a hundred years ago. Afterwards a woman came up to me. While I had been talking about the record-breaking, sweltering summer of 1911, when the wells had dried up and over-dressed Edwardians had gone half-crazy with heat, I had mentioned that one Essex man had been arrested for insanity after stripping stark naked as he walked the Braintree streets to work. The woman had suddenly remembered a previously forgotten incident. Perhaps it was the warmth of the tent, or the flowered print of my summer dress, or simply my spoken-out-loud description of that long-ago August day: she could not be sure. But something had jogged into her consciousness a long-submerged childhood conversation, when her grandmother had recounted an anecdote from her wedding day. Her cotton wedding dress was covered in a pattern of lilac-coloured pansies. After the reception in the bride's family's garden, the moment came for the newlyweds to leave for their honeymoon, and although she had not changed out of her wedding dress, guests remarked on the elegant simplicity of the bride's going-away clothes. The intense strength of the sun, during that prelapsarian summer before the First War, had bleached the pansies clean away. Only now, one hundred years after the event, did her granddaughter remember and trust the veracity of her grandmother's story. There were tears in her eyes as she thanked me for the verbal madeleine.

The collapsing of time through anecdotal recollection is an exhilarating game. When my grandfather was a child he went on holiday to France and was introduced to a very old man with a long white beard who, as a child himself, had been the personal standard-bearer for Napoleon Bonaparte, stepping out at the front of the Emperor's procession as it made its way towards the battlefield at Waterloo. On another occasion the same grandfather had been holidaying in the Alps, walking through the summer mountain flowers with a couple of undergraduate friends. Taking shelter in a log cabin from a sudden cold wind, the young men fell to discussing the author of the novel they were all reading. Had Charlotte Brontë really loved Mr Nicholls, they wondered, or had her father pressed his bachelor curate on an unwilling daughter? An old man who had been sitting unobtrusively in the corner by the fire suddenly stirred. 'I can assure you all that Charlotte certainly married Mr Nicholls out of feelings of true love,' he told them sternly. 'And *I* should know the truth, because I *am* Mr Nicholls.'

Sometimes I ask myself, if I were to arrive in heaven now, which days of my life would be the most enjoyable to look back on, and to give the game more edge, which the least? The Christmas day when I was given my first bicycle? The day I wore my first mini skirt with its silver buttons? The day I first fell in love? The days on which my children were born? The day I failed my driving test? The day I passed my driving test? The day my father died? The day I knew why I wanted to marry again? The shape of this mental exercise, the often delicious immersion in nostalgia, is both familiar as well as constantly evolving. But when facing death itself, be it one's own or that of someone close, one becomes even more conscious of the simultaneous joy and sadness that comes with remembering. 'Men live by forgetting,' T.S. Eliot wrote, 'women live on memories.' For men who have lived through war this generalisation seems to hold true. Even the redoubtable Henry Allingham waited until his centenary year before he could bear to speak of the hellish trenches of the Great War.

In 1920 the poppy that had threaded its way through the corn and wheat fields of the Western

Front was adopted as the symbol of remembrance for those who died within sight of the scarlet flower. Blood-red poppies had been the last living thing so many of their friends ever saw. Now that even Henry Allingham is no longer here, there are no known living survivors of the Great War, but for some of those who lived on for ninety years after the guns stopped firing, the annual sight of those commemorative poppies brought back nothing but pain. The opening lines of *The Waste Land*, Eliot's great postwar poem, addresses memory's power to torment. In order to find a way of coping with its monumental tragedy, Britain had tried for the course of the war years to protect itself from too much suffering by denying the scale of the tragedy. 'Human kind/Cannot bear very much reality', Eliot wrote later in *Burnt Norton*, the first of his *Four Quartets*. And so the dark, wintry years of the 1914–18 conflict were at times kept paradoxically warm and optimistic, 'covering/Earth in forgetful snow'. For as long as the fighting continued there was always the hope that it might end soon, that those who were missing abroad might return, and even, in the absence of the repatriation of bodies, that loved ones might only be dead for the duration of the war. The springtime of Eliot's *Waste Land* is a paradoxically cruel season as it brings with it a reawakening of consciousness after a long, collective submerging of painful truth. With the aftermath of winter comes the unavoidable light of April, 'the cruellest month', from which it is impossible to hide. As a consequence it is necessary to face up to this new, arid landscape, 'mixing/Memory and desire, stirring/Dull roots with spring rain.'

Other than the death of a child, the loss of a parent can be the most unsettling of adult experiences, sometimes robbing one of the illusion that there is more of one's life left to be lived than has gone before. As long as a parent provides the ceiling above one's fragile emotional structure, one is protected from exposure to the winds that buffet those who must accept responsibility for themselves. Some of my most personal memories are rooted in the unique experience of living through and beyond the death of a parent. In just a few months I will be exactly the same age as my mother was when she died. Her own mother had succumbed to the same fatal disease at the same age: the track record for longevity on the maternal side of my family is unimpressive. I have been approaching this generational hurdle with a mixture of sadness and finger-crossing triumph. I feel sad knowing that my mother did not live to share the splendid adulthood of her grandchildren; that she missed visiting the lovely garden her son-in-law has made; and that, as a cheerleader for the monarchy, she will never witness the renaissance of a royal family who seemed down on their luck in the late 1980s when she died. Yet I feel miraculously fortunate that I am poised to outlast the life spans of both a parent and a grandmother. Although my mother had been ill for a while, the end came suddenly in a hospital bed, her fall into unconsciousness depriving me of the chance to say goodbye.

My father's death was an altogether different matter. During his last few months his existence narrowed to a distillation as well as a reflection of the way he had responded to life. Throughout their marriage my parents had occupied separate bedrooms; my mother slept alone in a double bed, and my father in a single. When my mother left to marry another man, my father continued to sleep in his monastic room. It was to this place that he climbed the stairs one final time after being diagnosed with an illness from which we all knew he would never recover. He lived for another eight months and he never again went downstairs or out into the garden that lay just below his window. Possibly the physical weakness that prevented him from walking there on his own was too distressing to acknowledge. Maybe he chose to save himself from the pain of saying goodbye to a place he had known and loved almost all his life. Or perhaps he could not bear the irony of dying in a place so vitally alive. Yet until the last day the room was a focus for all the things he had loved best. I now realise that his passions and dislikes could somehow be sifted according to his sensory habits. A lifetime's indifference to classical music was emphasised by his equally long-standing passion for popular songs from musicals like *Oklahoma!*, *South Pacific* and *My Fair Lady*. When a few years earlier he had been invited as a castaway on *Desert Island Discs*, he had taken as much trouble as anyone over his list of eight records, and was surprised and a little hurt at his friends' amusement following the broadcast programme. No one disputed the excellent choice of the haunting *Lily Marlene*, sung during the Second World War across no man's land by the enemy and returned in answering chorus by the British troops. It was a song that never failed to move my father to tears, no matter how often he heard it. The sentimental selections *I Could Have Danced All Night* and *A Nightingale Sang in Berkeley Square* were followed by a chart-topping pop record of the 1960s, sung by a girl who had a thing about not wearing shoes, which reminded him of the time when he was in unrequited love with a young American research assistant. Ravel's *Bolero* was included because it had accompanied Torvill and Dean's balletic performance on the ice and was the only piece of classical music my father could identify. The recording of Patricia Hodge reading from *Pride and Prejudice*, musical in cadence alone, certainly caused the odd raised eyebrow.

During those dying months, as the days grew warmer and the daylight hours stretched far into the evening various adjustments were made. An abstract painting by a granddaughter, a red-and-blue block of colour, was propped bedside his bed, as was a framed print of his favourite portrait, Gainsborough's *Mr and Mrs Andrews*. The television set was brought from downstairs and took up its position on the chest of drawers. This was 2004, the year of the Summer Olympics in

Athens. The combination of athletic beauty and a backdrop of his favourite city on earth provided him with something wonderful to watch, although a visit from his dearest friends or the sight of one of his own grandchildren's heads peering round the door to check he was not asleep satisfied his visual sense more than anything else. As this gradual closing-down of time persisted, I began to believe it would never end. And even though we failed to persuade him to go outside into the garden, he welcomed the arrival in his room of a bunch of miniature narcissi, or two or three grape hyacinths in a sherry glass. The scent of these spring flowers brought the promise of new life, and with it, hope. Beside his bed sat a series of tiny vases, the sort that my grandmother used to keep on her writing desk when she wanted to study the single stem of a flower for its shape or its perfume. My father's favourites were *Aquilegia*, with their jester caps of every colour, and sweet-smelling 'Madame Alfred Carrière', the first rose planted in the garden he had loved since the age of twelve.

Curiously taste, albeit frugal in quantity and restrained in scope, meant a great deal to him during those final few weeks. Here was a man whose ideal meal has been coincidentally replicated by Ian McEwan in his tale of marital disaster, *On Chesil Beach*, set in 1960. Whenever we went to France – to Paris to visit Napoleon's golden catafalque, to the battlefields of Normandy to wonder at the ranks of Kipling's stark headstones, or simply for a jaunt so we could say we had eaten breakfast in one country, lunch in another and dinner at home again – my father would always eat the same food in a restaurant. A glass of Dubonnet would be ordered in an exaggerated French accent to make us children laugh. Somehow it was the most suggestive word I ever heard him use.

After the sticky, sweet drink, a McEwan-style 'wedge of unripe melon decorated with cherry' would arrive, followed by a steak '*très bien cuit, s'il vous plaît*'. He would finish up with crème caramel, or if that was unavailable, another slice of melon. Melon and steak were dishes only to be served in paying establishments, and therefore never appeared on the dining-room table at home or made that final journey up to his bedroom. But as the end approached, three raspberries popped in the mouth seemed, at least for a day or two, to contain a life-giving elixir.

With this concentration of pleasure came expressions of regret, about memories he knew he would now never have of places he had never visited. Allied with the regrets came a new honesty. Sex troubled him. Like Betjeman, he felt he had not had enough of it, or ever succeeded in being very good at the whole enigmatic process. He felt he had loved too often but never too well. Sex, that most encompassing of all sensory experiences, when the hippocampus is aroused into complete response, remained for my father unsatisfyingly mysterious, even somehow shameful. Confined to his single, starchy-sheeted bed, my father continued to be as physically self-conscious and reserved as ever, flinching apologetically if someone crossed the line and stroked his hand, yet occasionally ruffling my hair as he used to do when I was a child as I bent to kiss him on the cheek. 'You must have three great loves in your life,' he told me once casually over the washing up. 'You need not marry all or, indeed, any of them, but while you are involved in these relationships they must be all-consuming.' At the end of his own life, however, he confided that he had been unable to consummate, as it were, his own advice. This failure assumed huge importance for him during those final months; and as he spoke with unprecedented openness, he wept for what might have been, for what should have been, lamenting the lack of chances to start all over again.

I pitied him, remembering the urgency of a meeting with the man I loved at a railway station in a tiny town in the South of France, a moonlit swim in the warm waters of the Mediterranean, and, at the culmination of a love affair, a garland of pale-pink roses threaded through an arch in a country churchyard. I felt blessed knowing that I would not share my father's regrets. Not that there was any doubt he had lived a rich and full life: several hundred people came to his memorial service – and listened to the Grenadier Guards band playing *Lily Marlene*.

The urge to transcend time becomes varyingly acute at different times in one's life. Each year, almost as soon as the summer light begins to fade, grown-ups start saying to each other, 'I can't believe it's nearly Christmas again. Doesn't time fly? Seems like only the other day I was sewing up that turkey.' Children roll their eyes, innocent of their parents' and grandparents' implicit lament. Linear time is hard to deny when one is faced with the evidence of a life well laughed indelibly marked around a mouth, or tired legs beginning to slow in their stride.

Memory can, of course, involve self-deception, and the temptation to exaggerate or sentimentalise the past is what gives nostalgia its bad name. Phrases such as 'in the olden days' and 'in my day' often herald unreliable comparisons with the present. The famously golden Edwardian summers that preceded the dark years of the First World War were in fact a product of elegiac myth. Apart from two sunny seasons in 1906 and 1911, the first thirteen summers of the twentieth century were notably damp and soggy; but it suited millions who craved the return of life before the conflict and tragedy to allow themselves a dab or two of the ointment of retrospective delusion. In two more lines from *Burnt Norton,* however, Eliot emphasises that with the very act of remembering comes an awareness of the now, and that honesty depends on living in the moment:

> 'What might have been and what has been
> Point to one end, which is always present.'

When someone much loved returns from a long absence abroad, words can wait. In the enclosing of one hand within another, a greater eloquence lies. On the last day of his life my father allowed me to take his hand in mine for the first time. Self-consciousness dissolved as trust and love were condensed and recognised in simple human contact. On that day, in that moment, memory had no valid part to play.